I'm Going to Crush Kindergarten

Written by Sonica Ellis

Illustrated by Nejla Shojaie

ISBN 979-8-9865281-4-4

D1519078

DEDICATION

This book is dedicated to all preschool graduates.
I know you are going to crush kindergarten!

It was the last week before preschool graduation. All the soon-to-be kindergartners gathered around, listening to Mrs. Mindy talk about what it was like in kindergarten.

Some of Mack's friends were a little anxious.
Some wanted to stay with Mrs. Mindy, but not Mack!

"Mrs. Mindy, I can't wait to crush kindergarten!" he said.
"My older brother and sister went to kindergarten, and they loved it.

"There are so many things to learn, and there are new games to play. I'm going to miss you, but I'm excited," Mack said. "I really can't wait to crush kindergarten."

"That's lovely! I know you're going to do amazing things in kindergarten, Mack." said Mrs. Mindy, giving him a big hug.

All the other kids who had been feeling anxious now felt hopeful.
They all wanted to crush kindergarten in their own way.

Preschool graduation came.

The students sang their songs and showed
their parents what they had learned in preschool.
Their parents all beamed with pride.

Mack said goodbye to his friends
and told them everything would be okay.

"Don't worry about kindergarten," he said.
"I know you're going to crush
kindergarten in no time!"

"But if you're a little unsure, my brother says the teachers are nice there," said Mack. "They helped him find his way. I'm sure they'll do the same for us."

They all said their goodbyes.

Summer came and went, but Mack was never afraid. He was so excited about being a big kid and going to kindergarten. He could hardly wait!

Mack went shopping with his mom for new clothes, a backpack, and other school supplies. They even bought some hand sanitizer to give to his teacher!

On day one, Mack rolled confidently into his new school.
He met his teacher, who was quite nice.

The teacher welcomed Mack. "My name is Mr. Ben," he said with a big smile.

"This will be your room as much as mine," said Mr. Ben. "This is a place where we will learn and have fun together."

Mack knew kindergarten was big,
but he didn't expect there to be
so many cool things to play with,
and so many new friends to make.

Mack saw a friend who looked a bit anxious, so Mack rolled over and introduced himself. "Hi, my name is Mack. You look like you might be a little nervous. Don't worry," he said. "I am sure that together you and I are going to

CRUSH
KINDERGARTEN!

The End

Made in United States
North Haven, CT
03 June 2023

37324229R00015